SPARKING ACADEMIC JOY

WRITING RETREATS FOR SCHOLARS

ANGELIQUE M. DAVIS
ROSE ERNST

ALCHEMY HOUSE PRESS

CONTENTS

Gratitude   v

PART I
INTRODUCTION
1. Breathe   3
2. Angelique's Story   5

PART II
JOY EXPONENTS
3. How Retreats Bring Joy   13

PART III
CHANGE YOUR MINDSET
4. Remove the Barriers   23

PART IV
DIAGNOSTICS
5. Diagnostic Test for Your Retreat   41
6. Diagnostic: Triage   42
7. Diagnostic: Proactive   44
8. Diagnostic: Inspire   52

PART V
CHOOSE YOUR OWN ADVENTURE
9. Details   59
10. Options for Triage Retreats   60
11. Options for Proactive Retreats   66
12. Options for Inspirational Retreats   80

PART VI
CONCLUSION

13. Rose's Story　　　　　　　　　　　　　　　89

PART VII
SAMPLE SCHEDULES
14. Triage Sample Schedules　　　　　　　　　93
15. Proactive Sample Schedules　　　　　　　 97
16. Inspire Sample Schedules　　　　　　　　100

PART VIII
TIPS FOR A SUCCESSFUL RETREAT
17. Angelique's Tips for a Joyful Retreat　　　107
18. Rose's Tips for a Joyful Retreat　　　　　 111

PART IX
RESOURCES AND FURTHER READING
19. Exhale: Online Writing Retreats　　　　　117
20. Exhale: Pause & Reset Academic Writing Retreats　　　　　　　　　　　　　　　119
21. Other Organized Retreats　　　　　　　　121
22. Retreat Centers　　　　　　　　　　　　 124
23. Recommended Books　　　　　　　　　　127
24. Retreat Databases　　　　　　　　　　　 131
25. Articles, Blogs and Additional Resources　133

About the Authors　　　　　　　　　　　　139

GRATITUDE

Angelique's Acknowledgments

I dedicate this book to my family and "village." First, there are not enough words to express the love and gratitude I have for my husband Cedric and his consistent support of me and my writing. For each of my children: Asia, Justice, CJ, and Georgia thank you for bringing so much joy into my life and understanding how writing retreats help me to be more present when I am with you. To my village—none of this could happen without you: Mom & Dad, Ramona & Rickey, Anna Fernandez, Candice Hightower, Darozyl Touch, Donna Tinner, Evelyn & Dion Cook, Jerrell Davis, and all of our other friends and family who help carry the load. The peace I have knowing my family is supported by you is priceless. I am forever grateful. To my Exhale Writing Retreat regulars Ayesha Hardaway, Daquiri Steele, Holly Ferraro, Jane Cross, Joya Hicks, Shakira Pleasant, Sharon Beckford-Foster, Susan Perkins, and Zenzele Isoke thanks for holding space with me to spark academic joy.

Rose's Acknowledgments

I would not be writing this book had it not been for Seva's encouragement to break out of the academic writing box and pursue independent publishing. Thank you for your unconditional love and support along the way to new chapters in my life. Mom, Dad, Ben, Baba, LaVonne, Randy, and little Tania have been my biggest cheerleaders; I'm particularly grateful for your acceptance of my health transitions and need to go on plenty of writing retreats! I also want to thank the Davis family for supporting Angelique in going on so many writing retreats with me. Finally, a major thanks to Meggin McIntosh for making the impossible seem perfectly easy.

Joint Acknowledgments

Many thanks to John Davis for his skillful editing assistance. We also want to thank the staff at the Whiteley Center for providing a such warm and welcoming space for writers. Most importantly, we want to thank Kathy Cowell, who has coordinated all of our stays at Whiteley and provided much joy and camaraderie along the way.

PART I

INTRODUCTION

1
BREATHE

Thank you for joining us to explore integrating joyful writing retreats into your academic life.

First, take a moment to breathe.

Imagine yourself looking out over the water, a slight breeze, and the feeling that you're on top of your writing projects.

This is how we feel when we go on writing retreats.

You can experience this, too.

...

Based on our research and experience, we've compiled materials to help you achieve the same benefits while avoiding our trial-and-error approach.

After dispensing with a few introductory matters, we explain the "why" of writing retreats and what we call *joy exponents*. Next, we discuss shifting your mindset about to retreats. We then turn to a discussion of what type of retreat you need. Finally, we'll share sample schedules and a few tips we've learned over the years.

2
ANGELIQUE'S STORY

I'm sitting on a patio outside of the study at my quarterly retreat location in the San Juan Islands. As I peer through the trees at the Salish Sea, birds chirping and the noise of falling water accompanying my stay, I reflect on how writing retreats have not only kept me productive as an academic but also sparked joy.

I've been "retreating" in some form or another for the past 15 years.

At first, it was an intermittent experience resulting from a pending pre-tenure deadline. While those retreats got the job done, I wouldn't say they sparked the same type of joy that my regular retreats that have become a part of my writing practice do. Over time, I coordinated with my partner weekend retreats at local hotels so I could accomplish larger chunks of uninterrupted writing.

These worked well for a time, but I realized I wanted something more than a trip here or there. I needed retreats as part of my writing practice.

I credit winning tenure with four children—three of whom joined our family while I was on the tenure track—to the National Center for Faculty Development & Diversity (NCFDD) and my writing retreats. While Kerry Ann Rockquemore is not a personal friend, I (like many other academics around the country) think of her as one. Her book, *The Black Academic's Guide to Winning Tenure—Without Losing Your Soul*, was given to me by a colleague when it was first published in 2008. As someone who transitioned from the legal profession, I searched for a by-the-rulebook on academic norms. In addition to teaching new preps, I was also beginning my research agenda and trying to figure out—let alone navigate—the tenure requirements at my institution.

Over time, my husband came to understand my need to "retreat" to get work done. Although I developed and maintained a daily writing practice, I still found the interruptions of family, institutional politics, and life in general often waylaid my best-laid writing plans. I found myself increasingly stressed and sleep deprived trying to manage it all. Moreover, even though I was accomplishing my writing goals with 30-minutes-a-day writing practice, I longed for time to delve deeper into my work. To wrestle with my work in a way that transitioning from writing to teaching to service to home didn't allow.

After the birth of our third child, a friend and colleague at another local institution told me about a retreat center designed solely for scholars. Located on San Juan Island, the Whiteley Center is owned and operated by the University of Washington as part of its Friday Harbor Laboratories property. One section of the center is used for classes and laboratories, and another part of the center is just for scholars.

My first retreat at the Whiteley Center was by myself. I stayed in a one-room cottage overlooking Friday Harbor. In addition to a well-appointed cottage, I also had a study equipped with all the things you need as a writer. This beautiful center was created to support this type of quiet contemplation and attracted scholars from around the world.

Since it was located so close to Seattle, where I live, I couldn't wait to share it with one of my colleagues, Rose Ernst. She had started at Seattle University a few years after me, and we both leaned on each other for support as junior faculty. I invited her on a retreat to the Whiteley Center in 2012, and the rest is history. We started going twice a year and now have a comfortable rhythm of going at the end of each academic quarter for a week. I can't imagine my scholarly life without it.

I started finding other ways to add retreats to my writing practice. I would add a few days onto a conference or get together with friends online. I found these experiences brought me joy, and when others heard about them, they were curious. Where did I go? How did I do them? How did that work with family and other responsibilities? Wasn't it too expensive?

Writers much more accomplished than I would perk up when they heard I regularly participated in writing retreats. What a lovely idea! Could I tell them more?

That is the impetus for this book. To explain not only why I take these retreats but also how. And, although the details are provided to get you started in figuring out how to structure your next retreat, I think the most beneficial aspect is the joy they've sparked in my writing as an academic.

I had a relatively enjoyable writing practice. I would light a candle, pour a warm beverage, and place a blanket over my lap. Take a few deep breaths and write. But it still felt like a heavy load. Part of my work I would avoid if I could. It felt like responding to interrogatories as an attorney. The passion was gone.

I tried writing at different locations, with local writing groups, and these all helped, but I felt like there was still something missing. I knew there were those who still loved to engage with their work. I remained passionate about it, but why couldn't I translate that to my writing practice?

And did contemplation need to be limited to a writing session in the morning and brief ruminations through the day as I ran from class to meetings to the grocery store to daycare through dinner, bath time, bedtime stories before collapsing in bed each night? I never felt fully present, no matter what I was doing. I'm sure the fact that my writing topics aren't conducive to writing for 30 minutes and then switching to getting my kids ready for school or feeling warm and patient to enter a class session. I write about racism. I write about the ugliness of the structural nature of white supremacy and its impact on the lived experiences of People of Color, which includes my family and me. I research and write about women whose children have been killed by police officers. Women like me. Thirty to sixty minutes of writing first thing in the morning before waking my kids up to go to school with a smile, breakfast, and hugs were too big of an emotional shift for me to make each day. It felt disjointed and chaotic.

I recognized that the transition was tough. So I started scheduling lighter projects for days I didn't have time to recharge after my writing sessions before re-emerging to the real world.

While my life wasn't conducive to long contemplative

writing sessions daily, I realized that this was something I could incorporate into my life. As I started charting the course of my professional aspirations, I tapped into my power to proactively create my writing practice in a way that inspired me.

For the past four years, I've gone on quarterly writing retreats. Most last for approximately a week or more and punctuate my year with opportunities for scholarly contemplation, writing, and whatever else I may need at that moment. While writing undergirds them all, they often have other objectives as well. Some are to triage an overwhelming number of projects and unreasonable commitments. Others to plan the upcoming term and make sure my commitments align with my goals. Some serve to recuperate from a rough term; I regroup and decide how to enter the academic space with my job intact.

Weeks when my entire family is sick with the flu, school is canceled, scores of papers and exams need to be graded, or other inevitable life interruptions take place, I still feel the stress. What is different now, that I didn't have before, is I know I will have the space I need to exhale, pause, and reset.

PART II

JOY EXPONENTS

3
HOW RETREATS BRING JOY

Writing retreats bring us joy in both expected and unexpected ways. This section includes reflections on the ways retreats can spark joy in your writing. This list is by no means exclusive, but rather an illustration of how the many facets of writing retreats interact to increase the joy we find in our work.

1. Pause and Reset

Joy has come to our lives as scholars because we regularly pause and reset. We use this metaphor to explain how we add mindfulness to our academic practice. Now, when we go on quarterly retreats, we not only advance a writing project but also take time to pause from the business of our everyday lives and reflect on where we are and where we're going. Are we using our time in a way that brings us joy? Are we using it the way we intended?

By pausing, we can take stock of what we've been doing and decide how we want to reset for the coming months. Often this includes removing things from our plates or reprioritizing a project we had put on the back burner. This can also mean intentionally creating more space for other things that bring joy, such as family and friends.

2. Health

Retreats help to center your health during your academic journey. And by health, we mean all facets of health that are important to you: mental, physical, spiritual, emotional. Academic life can be stressful! If you're pre-tenure, are you meeting the often elusive standard for tenure? You just received nasty reviewer comments. You've been asked to be on another committee, and although you're already maxed out with service, this is something you care about! Some of your colleagues are cray-cray and get away with it because they have tenure. You child was up with a fever the night before you had a peer review of your class. We're sure you can think of many things to add to this list.

All of these things take a toll on our health and our ability to write. The adage of "putting your oxygen mask on first," is hard to do. "I'll do it after …. [insert here: tenure, the quarter, I submit this article, etc.]." You may be fortunate and able to continue on like this, but many of us have been stopped in our tracks at the most inconvenient times due to health conditions! Life happens, even though we all try to avoid crises.

3. Control

While you can't always avoid a crisis, sometimes you can stop, or at least slow down, a train wreck. Sometimes we don't even recognize that there is about to be a catastrophe because we haven't slowed down enough to take stock of our situation. Or, you may see that something terrible is about to happen, but feel powerless to stop it. This is where controlling the things we can come in.

Through taking time to pause and reset, you can evaluate what things in your life you can control and what you can't. You can't change the deadline for your R&R (okay, you can ask for a few extensions, but you're going to have to get it done). You don't want to change the fact that you have a family (hope we're not assuming too much here). But you can change how you're going to interact with the cray-cray colleague we mentioned earlier. You can assess your service commitments and class assignments to determine if they align with your goals. You can regularly set aside time to devote to writing.

4. Momentum

Retreats are a fantastic way to maintain, increase, divert, interrupt, or create momentum. If you already have writing momentum, then this is the opportunity to maintain or increase it. Not only will you make significant progress on a writing project, but you may find that the pace of your project has picked up steam because you are giving it more attention.

On the flip side, think about the inevitable train wreck that we mentioned in the previous section. It's the result of loose ends picking up momentum. What if you had time to divert the disaster before it hit? Or stop the train wreck altogether? Have you considered how you can turn around that energy, so things are slowly building up momentum with your writing projects?

Or maybe you're stuck on a project that needs some momentum. Retreats are a fantastic way to propel a project forward. Your retreat can be used to familiarize or reacquaint yourself with a new project. And once you start and can see the next step, the train begins to roll.

. . .

5. Regroup

To avoid repeating earlier sections, we'll add that sometimes your scholarly life is so out of control you need time to pull yourself together and decide where you're going next. This could be the result of many factors, both personal and professional. Maybe your chair just told you that you need two more articles than expected for tenure or that something you'd been working on for the past few years didn't turn out as expected. Maybe that cray-cray colleague has been making you miserable. Retreats are an excellent find the space to pull yourself together.

6. Connect

Retreats are an excellent way to connect with other scholars. Later in this book, we'll talk about different ways you can use retreats to connect and find inspiration. The point here is that they don't have to be a solitary experience. Of course, you want to prioritize your own writing, but they can also be an excellent way to work with co-authors, spend time with friends from graduate school, your writing group or a facilitated experience that allows you to connect with others whose experiences uplift and inspire you.

. . .

7. *Rest & Recharge*

Everything looks brighter when we're rested. As we'll discuss later, proactively planned writing retreats are conducive to accomplishing work and resting! It sounds like an oxymoron, but we promise you it's not! You can take time to rest, write, and recharge if you plan your retreat with that in mind.

8. *Empowerment*

Making progress on our writing empowers us to not only do more but to *know* we can. We're going to write it one more time...read this slowly to let it sink in. Making progress on our writing empowers us to not only do more but to *know* we can. Like riding a bike, learning to read, cooking, you name it—once you start something and see your progress you are not only able to do that thing, but you know deep down that you can. This is the same with writing. Seeing significant progress with our writing empowers us to accomplish more. Because we see, we believe, and then are empowered because we *know* we can.

9. *Rewards*

A side benefit to retreats is the opportunity to reward

yourself for your accomplishments. Whether that's taking a walk, indulging in a show or movie, eating something yummy, or [insert reward you like here], retreats are a great way to get used to reinforcing our successes with a reward. And, if you need further justification research support that rewards are crucial to developing good habits. In *The Power of Habit*, Charles Duhigg explains how rewards are a necessary part of the cue-routine-reward loop of the habit formation process. Retreats create spaces to reward ourselves for writing in both small and large ways. This allows us to reinforce current habits and also develop new ones. Both of us enjoy taking long walks or coffee breaks on retreats (see retreat tips for further ideas).

10. Flow

According to positive psychologist Mihaly Csikszentmihalyi, flow is an autotelic experience—an activity that's pleasant, enjoyable, and intrinsically motivating. In relation to writing, this means that when you are in flow, you are completely absorbed, focused, and involved in your writing while also enjoying it. Imagine that! Retreats provide an optimal environment for flow by creating space that allows one to be completely absorbed in the joy of writing.

These joy multipliers typically do not happen all at

once. Depending on your needs at the time, they will occur in uniquely personal ways. After getting past all the mindset barriers of why you can't retreat in the next chapter, you will have the opportunity to diagnose the type of retreat you need in the short-term as well as develop a long-term plan for how you can incorporate writing retreats as part of your writing practice.

Ultimately, these joy multipliers work together to bring joy to your work as a writer. Our goal is to help you incorporate them into your life.

II. *Reinforces Identity as Writer*

Finally, writing retreats reinforce your identity as a writer in a low-stakes environment. Academic conferences and lectures provide opportunities for us to showcase our work but are high stakes. And we know that to get to that stage you have to do the hard work of butt-in-chair writing. The experience of writing retreats reinforces not only your academic identity but also your identity as a writer through the experience of consistently setting aside time and space to write. Instead of writing just to meet deadlines and clear academic hurdles, you create space to enjoy the writing process in and of itself.

PART III

CHANGE YOUR MINDSET

4

REMOVE THE BARRIERS

Over the years, Angelique and I have noticed that no matter how much we rave about our own retreats, people rarely follow through and go on their own.

We became curious about this and compiled a list of objections we've heard. Even if you're ready to go on a retreat, it's helpful to see these objections because they may creep up on you even during your retreat.

First Objection: I don't have the money.

This is one of the most common reactions to the idea of a writing retreat. Don't let lack of funds stop your writing retreat dream!

You can deal with a tight budget in a few ways.

1. Find a Low-Cost Option

As we cover in other sections, you have a few low-cost retreat options:

- **Friends or Family**

Though free, you'll want to approach this retreat with caution. Writing retreats rarely work if friends or family lurk around your space, even if you have a separate room. If you're sensitive to people's energy, it might be hard to focus even if you close the door. Chances are high they'll want to talk to you—or you'll seek them out as a distraction. A short 15-minute coffee break with them can turn into an hour of chatting!

Best option: Housesit for friends or family.

- **A Third Space**

A library, coffee shop, or hotel lobby can serve as free (minus the coffee expense) options for one- or two-day weekend retreats. A third space is especially appealing because it's easy to plan and doesn't depend on other's schedules.

- **Online Retreat**

Working with a colleague or co-author via Zoom or Skype is another free option. This works because you accompany each other in writing, even if it is in your respective homes. Use caution here, however, if you have family around the house. You need to make sure they know today is your writing retreat day.

2. Find Funding

- **Faculty Development Funds**

We are continually surprised by how many colleagues never inquire about using their faculty development funds for a writing retreat. We've funded our retreats with faculty development funds for years. Ask the administrator in charge of the funds whether you can use them for this purpose. This works particularly well if you've applied to a retreat center of a hosted retreat that appears more legitimate than renting a hotel room (even though we know the outcome can be the same).

You can also make a one-time case to your dean. This involves a deadline or goal the university wants you to achieve, such as tenure or becoming full professor. Tell your dean you have a writing retreat opportunity which will allow you to finish X project so that you can submit your file, for example. Will they offer support in moving you toward your goal? Note: this strategy works well if you have already applied to a retreat center or an organized retreat.

- **Conferences**

We've used a conference technique many times. Book your conference hotel a few days before or after your conference. Make those extra days your retreat days. You've saved airfare expenses, and you may be able to count those extra hotel nights as part of your conference travel, depending on your university's reimbursement restrictions.

- **Grants**

If you have a research grant, find out whether it covers research and writing time away. If you use the grant to conduct field research, consider using the conference technique discussed above—tack on a few days before or after your research trip as a writing retreat.

- **Tips for graduate students**

We know money is tight and it can seem frivolous to spend money on a writing retreat. But trust us, if you follow what we've laid out in this book, it will be worth it. Administrators can be persuaded to fund your retreat if you have a specific outcome attached to it. For example, if you're a graduate student, you might approach your chair or the chair of the department. Here's a sample script of what you might say (please note this works toward the end of your graduate career):

"I'm on track to finish my dissertation by the end of this academic year as I'm planning to go on the market in the fall. I applied to X retreat space and if I am accepted, would you consider supporting a research/writing retreat so I can complete my project on time?"

- **Professors without development funds**

If you're a contingent faculty member or work at a community college, finding funding may be more difficult. If you're at a teaching institution, however, you can make a similar case to your chair or dean about supporting finishing a pedagogy article for publication, for example. You might be working on research that can bring positive attention to the university. Tell them about this; you need space and time to finish it for publication in a non-academic venue. It's worth a try!

Second Objection: I should spend this money on other academic priorities.

This requires a significant shift in your mindset.

- How much is your Ph.D. worth?
- How much is tenure worth?
- How much is it worth to share your brilliance with the world?
- How much is your sense of connection to your work worth?
- How much is your physical, spiritual, mental, and emotional health worth?

The fact that these elements of your career are not able to be measured does not mean you should ignore these questions. We're not suggesting that one writing retreat will get you tenure, but it is part of paying yourself first, as Kerry Ann Rockquemore says.

Questions to consider:

- How many conferences do you really need to go to a year? Can you be selective and use your money one year for a retreat?
- Can you tack on a few extra days to your conference and have your own retreat?
- Would you like some joy and spaciousness in your academic life?

Third Objection: *I don't have the time.*

Leaving aside caregiving responsibilities discussed in a later section, colleagues often say "they don't have the time for a retreat" as if it is a luxurious undertaking. While we certainly luxuriate in the spaciousness of time, we do not consider it a luxury (we hear the money objections—look at the questions about that for resources on low-cost and free retreats). If you need to produce scholarship for your job, then this is *part of your job*. And do you find your service and teaching obligations declining over time?

No, we didn't think so.

No one would object to us traveling to a pedagogy workshop or a work 'retreat' for an exhausting service obligation. And they certainly wouldn't consider it frivolous! If your scholarship is a frivolous pursuit, then perhaps you don't have the time for the retreat. If it is part of your job, then it is scarcely frivolous, which is why we advocate asking your university to pay for it (see other section on money).

Fourth Objection: I'm too tired.

Tara Mohr, author of *Playing Big*, asks, "Am I just too tired to play big right now?" Without going into the details of Mohr's book (fabulous), we've found this objection is often an easy, knee-jerk way to dismiss a writing retreat. What gets ignored, however, is that your exhaustion may mask larger academic work issues worth exploring. Mohr says, "We think playing big will drain us, but playing small is far more draining."

Paying yourself first by taking a writing retreat is part of this playing big ("being more loyal to your dreams than your fears"). If you are exhausted—and we know so many academics are—then make sure you plan a slightly longer retreat to rest! Rest is absolutely integral to most writing retreats.

Being away from your normal routine will not only allow for rest, but will also allow you to consider new ways to delegate and draw boundaries at home, work, and in community. How can you finish your scholarship without tiring yourself out even more? Can you decline some service activities? Can you delegate some teaching tasks?

In other words, exhaustion is *exactly why* you need a writing retreat.

Fifth Objection: I don't want to be alone with myself that long.

A widely cited 2014 study titled "Just Think: The Challenges of the Disengaged Mind," psychologist Timothy

D. Wilson and his colleagues reported the following findings:

"In 11 studies, we found that participants typically did not enjoy spending 6 to 15 minutes in a room by themselves with nothing to do but think, that they enjoyed doing mundane external activities much more, and that many preferred to administer electric shocks to themselves instead of being left alone with their thoughts. Most people seem to prefer to be doing something rather than nothing, even if that something is negative." (75)

Wilson et al.'s results point to a deeper mindset issue—one that you may not want to consider. This is an objection we've heard behind the other objections to writing retreats and is one that we've struggled with ourselves. Even if we enjoy getting lost in our own thoughts, most people struggle with distraction, regardless of whether they are happy to be alone. This is particularly true when it comes to digital distraction.

A week-long writing retreat can be an antidote to distraction, but you may subconsciously avoid one because you fear being alone with painful thoughts. Or perhaps you're aware that you struggle to sit down and write. Another reason might be that your work is emotionally draining and personal. We get it!

The beauty of a retreat is that acknowledging these

thoughts means you can address them on your retreat, or simply practice being alone—possibly with a digital detox. The key is to be gentle and plan for these diversions, as we discuss later.

Like with many things in life, the fear of being alone or distracted is worse than the reality. If you're used to pushing hard all the time, it may take a day or two to unwind and settle into a space where your mind can focus. Once you do, however, you may find that you never want to go home!

Sixth Objection: I'm overwhelmed by my options.

Absolutely! That's why we wrote this book. Planning a retreat is like fitting together a jigsaw puzzle. You may have decided you want to rent a cabin on the beach for a week, but you don't know what to bring or what to plan for before you go. Similarly, you may need to finish an article and need a distraction-free space to complete it, but you don't know how long you'll need or where you should go. If this is your primary challenge, we suggest you skip ahead to the diagnostic section of the book so you can get started on concrete planning tasks.

Seventh Objection: I'm afraid I will waste my retreat time.

Retreats can have an odd internal FOMO quality, similar to a brief vacation. You book a week somewhere with lofty plans to finish three projects (writing retreat) or to relax (vacation) but as soon as you arrive, you have a sense that the time has already ebbed away. That's why setting intentions for your retreat is so important. This could entail specific writing goals or just a plan for what you'll do each day—even if that means planning to do nothing but wander and think.

Consider Alex Soojung-Pang's thoughts on routine and freedom in his book, *Rest: Why You Get More Done When You Work Less*: "Routinization of work, the researchers concluded, does not have to diminish creativity; if it's accompanied by freedom, routine can enhance creativity."

Unless you are in emergency triage mode (see the diagnostic section), it's fine that you plan your retreat time to wander and think about your projects or long-term writing/career intentions. What matters is that you allow yourself the time to do that and not worry you should be doing something else.

Eighth Objection: It sounds great, but I'm not sure what I'll get out of it.

We are still amazed by what we accomplish on a retreat,

even after going many times. We cannot quantify these accomplishments—it actually feels magical when we realize what we've done. This happens the most when we're clear about what we want to accomplish *before* we go on retreat. Don't overload your schedule (unless you're in triage mode, but even then you need to be very clear about your goals) so you have plenty of time to rest, exercise, and wander.

One of the reasons writing retreats are so magical is because our days are not filled with distractions, both welcome and unwelcome. We're not doing laundry, preparing elaborate meals, meeting someone for coffee, shuttling kids around to appointments, checking email incessantly, responding to various crises (both real and imagined) and so forth. We're not saying that you should eliminate all of these things when you return from your retreat, but it does give you some clarity about what you can actually accomplish when you eliminate some distractions. This has the welcome secondary effect of helping you to identify which of your daily or weekly activities/tasks you can eliminate, minimize, or delegate!

Ninth Objection: *I have too many service activities.*

Time for boundaries! Both of us have had these realizations on retreats. We overload our schedules with meetings, coffees, committee meetings, long phone calls, or long email sessions related to our service work. One of the best things you can practice on a writing retreat is to be unavailable, except to those who are most dear to you (it's your call on how available you'll be during the retreat).

Something odd happens when you leave a space where you're taken for granted, which is often the case for underrepresented faculty who are called to take on more than their fair share of university service. First, you realize how much of your time is taken up by those activities, which will hopefully spur you to eliminate, minimize, or delegate some of those activities. Second, you realize which activities can run along without you and which fall apart. Third, people may come to appreciate you a bit more when you're not available all the time. The more unavailable you become, the more people respect you because they think you have big plans!

Tenth Objection: I'm afraid I'll never want to go back to normal life!

It's so true! Sometimes it's hard to go back, but that is a welcome if sometimes uncomfortable opportunity to reflect on why that is. Perhaps you're happy to see your family, but not go back to the university. If that's the case, what can you do to make your work life more bearable, more fulfilling, or dare we say, more joyful?

Eleventh Objection: I have kids, or I'm a primary caregiver. I cannot leave them.

Angelique here. This one is highly personal. To honor how individualized our particular situations are I am going to share my thoughts with you on how I navigated this. I'm hoping part of this will resonate with you, but it may not. In either case, if this is a barrier, I gently urge you to consider your options.

Before I started regular retreats, I frequently felt distracted when I was with my family because I felt I "should" have been writing. This is a common dilemma —being torn between work and family responsibilities. This resulted in me waking up in the wee hours of the morning to write (including right after I returned home after my son's birth), or during nap time on the days I didn't have childcare, and I was beyond exhausted.

The adage to "put on your own oxygen mask first," hit home the day I drove through a red light with my kids in the car. I didn't realize what I'd done until one of my children asked, "Mommy, why didn't you stop at the red light?" We're blessed that nothing happened, but that scared me enough to examine how I was working.

My family misses me when I'm away, and I miss them. But I'm a more present and joy-filled mother and partner because I regularly take time for myself and my writing. My children know when it's time for mommy's writing retreat. Not long ago I overheard my six-year-old lamenting that I had to go on the retreat and my nine-year-old replied, "if she doesn't go we won't get to see her as much when she's here!"

Most of us attend conferences and have other travel related to our work. While we might wish we were home (I, in fact, miss my family but will level with you that I love having a hotel room all to myself) this is a part of our profession. Moreover, many other professions also include travel and caretakers occupy those positions. My partner's previous position required 30-40% travel. He was away on a regular basis, and we accepted it as part of his professional obligations. Writing retreats are part of mine.

Writing retreats allow me not only to write but decide how I'm going to approach my writing for the upcoming quarter in relation to my care-taking and other responsibilities. This allows me to experience the joy exponents we discussed earlier. In addition, I think my partner appreciates me more when I get home.

Twelfth Objection: *I have a lot of health issues.*

If you are managing health issues that alone is reason enough to take writing retreats. It can be difficult to manage your health and all the obligations of academic life. Often personal care is the first thing to go when we're busy. Writing retreats not only offer the space to write, but also to manage our health.

We both deal with a number of health issues and have found our health has improved as a result of taking writing retreats. They reduce our stress. Angelique named her residential retreats *Exhale: Pause and Reset*, because this is literally what she does on her retreats. They allow her to hit a metaphorical pause button by making her unavailable, and give her the opportunity to reset. Resetting includes how she is going to manage her health given the demands on her time.

While health issues may impact where you choose to retreat, we hope they don't discourage you from trying them. If you are able to travel for other reasons while managing your health, utilize those same strategies to approach participating in a writing retreat.

PART IV

DIAGNOSTICS

5

DIAGNOSTIC TEST FOR YOUR RETREAT

Now that you've blown through mindset blocks, let's figure out what kind of retreat you need!

Broadly speaking, there are three kinds of writing retreats: triage, proactive, and inspirational. Understanding what you need is essential. If you go on a triage retreat with a loose plan, however, you'll find yourself disappointed and frustrated by how little you've accomplished. In contrast, if you're exhausted, mentally, physically, emotionally, or spiritually, and overschedule your retreat, you'll return home even more burned out then when you arrived!

We recommend that you approach this next section by identifying which kind of retreat you need and then skip ahead to find out more about that retreat in Part V.

6

DIAGNOSTIC: TRIAGE

As Kerry Ann says, "All your shit, ain't gonna fit." That is true in general, particularly when we've taken on too many responsibilities. But what about those times when the shit not only doesn't fit, but it's also about to hit the fan? Or it has, and you're in clean-up mode?

You need a triage retreat if: you have a deadline(s) within the next month that you won't be able to meet without a significant intervention or miracle; you're frozen like a deer in headlights because you have too many tasks that needed to be completed yesterday; you have an important review on the horizon and need to have an article(s) submitted; or [insert your own academic emergency].

Triage retreats are by no means optimal, and we recommend avoiding them if at all possible. They don't provide time for reflection, planning, inspiration, or rest. There isn't much joy while you're on a triage retreat. As the saying goes, "The joy comes in the morning." Here, your joyful morning comes when you've met your deadline.

7

DIAGNOSTIC: PROACTIVE

The proactive category is an ideal place to be when planning a writing retreat. It's definitely less stressful than a triage retreat but can quickly become stressful if you haven't planned your intentions in advance. This is the kind of retreat where you can feel that you've wasted time or don't have enough time if you haven't thought about what you'll do in advance.

Having intentions does not mean, however, that you have to work around the clock or not have time for spontaneous walks and naps! It means the opposite because you've already planned generally for those things—how detailed that plan is will be a personal preference. If you're someone who plans everything down to the minute, however, this might be a time to let up on that plan. Similarly, if you're someone who thinks planning is constricting, you might experiment (just a little) with a more structured day to see what you can accomplish.

The following steps lay out diagnostic questions to find out whether your retreat fits the proactive category. If it does, then you'll want to skip ahead after this section to read the proactive section to find out more details about *how* to plan a proactive retreat.

1. Do you need to plan a project?

Perhaps you need one more article before you're ready for tenure or promotion. Or perhaps your dissertation chair said you need one extra chapter before you're ready to defend.

If so, you're ready for a proactive planning retreat. We love these kinds of retreats because they have a built-in thinking/dreaming component, but also have defined boundaries so you cannot get too lost along the way. You may have an idea for a new article, chapter, or book, but need time away to think it through.

In this case, plan on at least two or more days away. Because you're in a ruminating stage, going to a beautiful place where you'll want to get outside is of particular benefit.

This kind of retreat can feel too short, especially if you don't create basic guidelines before you arrive. Ask yourself how much time you'd like to devote to thinking, research, and writing? What is your goal for the end of the retreat? Try set an easy goal so that if you achieve it, you'll be happy. In this kind of scenario, it's easy to overpromise that you'll figure out everything you need to start the project. Set it up so you can continue the momentum you've gained from the retreat when you return home.

2. *Start a project—get going*

Let's say you've already planned your project (above), but just need to get going on it. This is also a perfect scenario for a proactive retreat.

Here are two scenarios:

- **I need to plan!**

You've already planned what your project is about and have a basic outline, but now you need to create more detailed steps about how to actually put this plan into action (See Meggin McIntosh's fantastic *Hunks, Chunks, and Bites* course). Perhaps you'll create a backward timeline to figure out how long this project will take and what steps you need to take to complete it. In this scenario, you plan to arrive home with concrete steps about what you need to do over the next few months to a year (or more!). This is wonderful because you don't have to worry about *doing* the project right now—that's for your future self!

- **I need to start!**

In this case, you've already created a plan, but you're not ready to start writing. This might involve reading, researching, and thinking in iterate loops. Make sure you set intentions around this before the retreat. If you engage in magical thinking that you'll have a draft of the paper when you leave the retreat, you'll be disappointed! Make sure you structure your day so you have plenty of time to read, research, and think.

3. Butt-in-chair drafting

This is self-explanatory. If you need to knock out a whole draft of a chapter or article, plan how you're going to accomplish this before you arrive. A drafting retreat can be one of the most rewarding kinds of retreats, but it requires that you really know your own writing style. If you're a slow-and-steady writer rather than one who writes in bursts (not that you can't be both), then plan for that before you go. Even if you write in bursts, you'll still want to make sure you plan plenty of time for breaks and rest at this kind of retreat so you don't arrive home exhausted.

Rather than writing via time blocks (the Pomodoro Technique, for example), we recommend using a word-count method for first drafting. This is because our inner critic or inner editor can derail us, even if we put in the time we allotted for that day. If your subconscious knows you're not finished until you write 1000 or 2000 words for the day, you're much less likely to stare out at the beautiful landscape ruminating about the right choice of words (see our resources section for more ideas).

4. Finish and submit

Along with butt-in-chair drafting, a finish-and-submit retreat is among the most satisfying. You arrive home feeling rested *and* accomplished! This retreat requires planning, especially because we often underestimate the time it actually takes to finish. For example, are you planning on editing it before you leave the retreat (perhaps you should hire an editor!), or are you going to write your submission letter to the journal and or submit it to the journal itself? Do you need to clean up your references? These fairly simple tasks often take longer than you anticipate. So plan for it!

5. *Assess and Reflect on big-picture goals*

Retreats offer the time and mental space for reflection on a grand scale. Perhaps you're in the middle of your dissertation and want to plan the next year so you can defend on time. Perhaps you're three years into the tenure process and need to assess your scholarship, teaching, and service priorities. Perhaps you need to examine your productivity, or publishing pipeline. Perhaps you've just won tenure and want to plan the next chapter in your scholarly career.

Some of these scenarios are more concrete than others. Defending your dissertation and winning tenure are time-bound goals. Planning a new chapter in your scholarly career is not, however. That means you'll want to be sensitive to how you structure your time on the retreat. If you want to spend it on freewriting and thinking, then make sure you plan for that so you feel satisfied when you arrive home, even if you have very little on paper.

6. *Learn/practice a new writing skill*

What? Learn a new skill? Or perhaps a writing skill you should have learned in graduate school? Yes! It will pay off in the near and long term. For example, Rose realized after she won tenure that the reason she struggled with editing her own work was because she had never been taught how to edit in graduate school. She researched and tried out new techniques on a chapter of her book. Though it meant the process took much longer than it needed to initially, that time she spent trying out different editing techniques saved her enormous amounts of time over the long run because she now had a method for self-editing her work. Hurray!

Another example could be learning how to write in a different form or genre. Many of us want to share our academic work with the world but struggle with translating it into language that is easily digestible and relevant for the general public. Perhaps you can devote your retreat time to learning how to write memoir, creative non-fiction, an Op-ed, or a blog.

7. *Need space with authors to work on a project*

One of the challenges of co-authoring is finding time to meet together to discuss your projects in depth, to discuss the big picture if you're working on a book project, or to write a grant together. A retreat is ideal for co-authors because you can come out of it with significant results. We certainly have. The key is to have clarity about your process and flow. If one of you gets up early and goes to bed early, while the other does the opposite, then you need to plan your day accordingly so one of you isn't sitting around because they're waiting for you to finish the next draft.

It's also helpful to decide how much time you'll spend together and whether or not you want to use your break time to discuss the project (e.g., meals and walks). There are definite benefits to being "in it" for the whole time because you're really inhabiting the project in a way you both cannot do when you're at home. On the other hand, knowing your limits is important because you can quickly burn out if the discussion and writing time are too intense. Know yourselves and know each other before you go!

8

DIAGNOSTIC: INSPIRE

Do you need joy in your academic life? We're not talking about reading the most cited scholar in your field and daydreaming you will one day be as sought after as they are. We mean something is missing, and you feel it regularly. Below are some common reasons why academics need writing retreats that inspire joy.

1. *"The Joy is Gone"*

As a child, when Angelique would complain about something being routine or boring, her father would quote a line from B.B. King's rendition of 'The Thrill is Gone." Now she substitutes joy for thrill into the lyrics and on bad days sings, "the joy is gone," to herself.

Depending upon the stage of your career, you will relate differently to this section. For a lucky few, the joy remains throughout their academic careers. For many, particularly after tenure, the realities of the academy begin to take their toll. Isolation, resentment, alienation, or some other form of disillusion compound. Many feel disconnected and check out or leave the academy altogether. For those who haven't disconnected or checked-out, they still need something to reignite them. If this explains you, you need an inspiration retreat to help find ways to bring joy back into your career.

2. *Keep Momentum*

An inspiration retreat can also be an excellent way to keep up the momentum with your writing by replacing the routine with something novel. For example, many runners will do destination marathons to add a new goal and novelty to their running. Many yoga practitioners go on yoga retreats to deepen their practice. This is true for many activities, including writing. An inspiration retreat will add some novelty to your writing practice that helps you keep up your momentum.

3. *Celebrate*

A celebration retreat is another way to inspire your

writing practice. Is there a significant milestone or goal to celebrate? This could be in relation to your writing or not. For example, you may want to go on a celebration retreat for your birthday and write a bit each day at a beautiful location. Maybe you're doing the final proofs on your book manuscript, and you want to celebrate your success by working on them while on a retreat. There are many ways you can use a writing retreat to celebrate your accomplishments or milestones that also inspire you to write.

4. Learn new approaches to writing

Are you wanting to change the direction of your writing? Maybe you're switching from doing mostly articles to writing essays or pieces for the popular press. Time to concentrate on learning a new approach to writing can be time-consuming and often daunting. A retreat is the perfect place to tackle this type of project.

5. Purpose

Another reason for an inspiration retreat is to reignite or find new purpose in your work. Why are you doing it in the first place? Back when you were naive to the realities of academia, what were you hoping to do? Who were you hoping to impact? What would your younger self think of what you're doing now? It's so easy to lose this perspective when focusing on tenure and promotion requirements, impact factor, reviewer comments, or other aspects of academic writing.

Or maybe you've achieved your objectives and are looking for a new purpose in your work. What do you really want to do now? We can become stuck in a rut and can't see a new direction. Some numb themselves because the joy is gone, and they long to feel excited about it again. If these statements resonate, an inspiration retreat is in order.

6. Supportive community

Writing retreats can also inspire joy through being part of a supportive community of writers. Writing with others brings energy to writing. Being around others who applaud you for finishing a writing sprint, your lit review, or another goal brings companionship and energy to what is often a solitary task. Those with whom you are writing don't need to have work related to your area in any way. What they do require, however, is an understanding of the joys and sorrows of academic writing.

7. Like-minded scholars

Retreating with a group of like-minded scholars in your field, with similar cultural backgrounds, or other affinities such as doing anti-racist work, is another way to spark academic joy. Most of us are the only or one of a few people doing similar work on our campus. And even if we keep up with others via email, telephone, and conferences our interactions are brief and often don't allow time for sustained conversation and exploration of new and innovative ways to approach our work. This is where an inspiration retreat comes in. Not only do you accomplish your writing with the energy and encouragement of your co-writers, but you also are encouraged in ways that specifically relate to, and inspire, you.

PART V

CHOOSE YOUR OWN ADVENTURE

9
DETAILS

Now that you've decided what kind of retreat you need, it's time to dive into the juicy details. We discuss the best venues for each option, along with budget and travel constraints.

10

OPTIONS FOR TRIAGE RETREATS

Here are the best options for a triage retreat.

1. Online

Budget: Free to $

Online retreats, facilitated or DIY, are another way to engage in a triage retreat that provides an additional layer of accountability and accompaniment. Options such as *Exhale: Online Writing Retreats* or setting up a Zoom session with colleagues can help to focus your efforts.

2. Conference or Trip Extensions

Budget: Free (reimbursed) to $$

Trip extensions are another way to incorporate triage retreats. By trip extension, we're referring to adding time before or after a work-related trip such as a conference or talk to focus on your writing. You're already out of town and hopefully, have set the expectation that you are will be unavailable due to your travel obligations. Why not extend your travel a bit to make space for your writing?

Benefits of adding time on the front end include extra time to prepare for your conference or talk. It avoids the rush of flying in at the last minute and the risk of being discombobulated by travel distractions. It can also provide time to work on a longer-term project that you need time to focus on.

Adding time at the end of a trip has its own benefits. You can incorporate feedback from the conference into your research while it is still fresh. The space afforded by extending your unavailability is also helpful to make additional time. This also allows you to re-enter your regular schedule without feeling behind.

This kind of retreat also provides opportunities to work with collaborators in person if all are attending the same event.

. . .

3. Hotel

Budget: Free (reimbursed) to $$$

Holing up in a hotel is a great way to have a triage retreat. Whether it's for the weekend or a week, staying in a hotel where you minimize distractions and can also have food readily available provides the opportunity to focus on your work. The length of your stay is, of course, dictated by your project and how much time you can get away.

There are different opinions on the type of hotel you should stay in. Some advocate for a no-frills hotel room that you wouldn't want to stay in for long so that you focus on getting your work done, not relaxing. Others find a more plush environment suitable to counter the pain of holing themselves up for days on end to finish their projects. Your taste and budget will dictate this choice.

Angelique went on triage retreats early in her career. During this time she was on the tenure track and adding children numbers 2 through 4 to her family. At that point, she hadn't yet figured out her writing practice and dealt with very unpredictable schedules with young children. She doesn't recommend them but did find them helpful to make space for her to finish projects on a tight timeline. This was something she worked out with her partner to help ease the stress of their dual-career household. She preferred to stay in the nicest hotel available for her budget and take advantage of room service!

Budget option: look for discounted hotels in your area. There are often last-minute deals due to excess inventory.

Caregiver tip: stay far enough away that you have to think about whether or not you really have to go home. For Angelique, this is typically at least a 90-minute drive from home.

4. Friends or Family

Budget: Free to $

Retreating with friends or family is also a great way to go on a triage retreat—if they understand that you must write. Hiding away at a friend or family member's home can provide a change of environment that minimizes the distractions of being in your own space. It's their home projects, so less urgency surrounds them on a personal level.

Believe it or not, some friends and family are appreciative of ways to support our work. Often it's challenging to know what to ask for when they offer to help. This may be an option. Using their home or vacation space to make progress on your writing projects can help them feel included in the process as well.

5. Local Options

Budget: Free to $

Local spaces where you can get away from everyday distractions and demands also provide opportunities for triage retreats. Instead of going to the office for the day or morning, instead, go to a space in your area that inspires you to write and where people can't easily find you. To truly retreat the coffee shop near campus is probably not the best space. Select a coffee shop, library, office building, even a hotel lobby that is far enough away from campus and/or your community where you're unlikely to have many interruptions.

Both of us have local spaces we use for mini-triage retreats. While we don't need them much, pre-identifying a space conducive for a triage retreat in your area is a vital tool to have in your writing toolbox. Angelique has a few coffee shops and library spaces and lobbies she uses in Seattle to chunk out larger blocks of uninterrupted time to finish a project. While she enjoys her home office, daily responsibilities sometimes interfere.

For example, her children could be on break from school, and the nanny is watching them at the house. Other times there have been home renovations or obligations taking her out away from her preferred home office. In this way, she can fit these mini triage retreats into her schedule.

11

OPTIONS FOR PROACTIVE RETREATS

Here are the best kind of projects for a proactive retreat:

- Start a project—get going
- Butt-in-chair drafting
- Finish and submit
- Assess and Reflect on big-picture goals (e.g., tenure file)
- Learn/practice a new writing skill
- Need space with authors to work on a project

We outline retreat-type details in the following sections. Though we do not discuss location extensively, we find 'nature' retreats most rejuvenating due to the healing properties of clean air, being near water, and/or resting in a quiet forest. Perhaps you find the city stimulating, however, which might be just what you need for your retreat. It all depends on your personality; we encourage you not to make this an afterthought, even if you plan to stay inside most of the time. In our experience, the difference between city and nature retreats is significant and is, therefore, an important consideration when designing your retreat.

1. Online

Budget: Free to $

Ideal for these intentions:

- Start a project—get going
- Butt-in-chair drafting
- Finish and submit
- Need space with authors to work on a project

Less ideal for these intentions:

- Assess and Reflect on big-picture goals (e.g., tenure file)
- Learn/practice a new writing skill

Online retreat advantages include minimal planning and monetary costs. You do not lose time due to travel. You can host your own with a writing group or a colleague by working on Zoom or Skype together. An online retreat could include simply setting a time and deciding to text one another, though this may be less effective than a digital face-to-face retreat. It depends on you, the participants, and the kind of projects you might be working on! If you're highly motivated to finish and not facing much resistance, then simply setting aside the time and checking in can work.

If, however, you expect a great deal of writing resistance to pop up, then joining an organized online retreat (see Exhale: Online Writing Retreats at the end of the book), might be best. If you have a four-hour period designated for the retreat and having someone else leading it, then all you do is show up and do the work (which is certainly more than enough)!

As is the case with all writing retreats, plans, and intentions are crucial. You don't want to arrive at your retreat not knowing what you're going to do because you'll use valuable brainpower trying to figure that out (see decision-fatigue). Arrive ready to do the work and have plenty of water and treats nearby so you can take breaks and reward yourself at the appointed time during the online retreat.

Online retreats are also great for jump-starting a project in the middle of the semester or quarter when you feel behind. They can help you regain writing momentum and inspire you to take a longer away-from-home writing retreat in the future.

2. Local

Budget: Free to $

Ideal for these intentions:

- Start a project—get going
- Butt-in-chair drafting
- Finish and submit
- Need space with authors to work on a project

Less ideal for these intentions:

- Assess and Reflect on big-picture goals (e.g., tenure file)
- Learn/practice a new writing skill

Local writing retreat locations include coffee shops, hotel lobbies, libraries, or other semi-public spaces. If you find it difficult to work at home because you suddenly want to clean the fridge whenever *that* literature review rears its head, then a local retreat can work well. This retreat has the advantage of being away from people who might lovingly and unintentionally distract you (this also means coffee shop where you know everyone might not be a great idea).

Costs are low, ranging from free (library or hotel lobby) to the price of a cup of coffee.

If you are co-authoring an article, local retreats can also be an ideal solution for working in writing sprints interspersed with short meetings. Again, you'll need to set your intentions beforehand because time slips away if you're catching up (necessary but should be brief) or planning what it is you should be already doing during the retreat time. Like an online retreat, you may be motivated by working next to someone, especially knowing that you're both advancing the same project!

These retreats are less ideal for learning new skills or assessing and reflecting on larger goals. It can be done, of course, but we find that truly being "away" is more conducive to reflection, assessment, and the goal of learning a new skill.

3. Friends and Family

Budget: Free

Ideal for these intentions:

- Start a project—get going

- Butt-in-chair drafting
- Finish and submit

Less ideal for these intentions:

- Assess and Reflect on big-picture goals (e.g., tenure file)
- Learn/practice a new writing skill
- Need space with authors to work on a project

Even if friends and family don't understand what you do all day, they want you (hopefully) to succeed! Can you housesit for someone while they're at a conference? Does a family member have a vacant room sitting? Does a co-author want to invite you over for a day (while their family is gone)?

These are ideal writing retreat scenarios, but they come with a caveat. If your mom agrees to let you write in the spare bedroom, be sure she understands you cannot be disturbed. She wants to socialize, and maybe you'll get in only one hour of writing. We've all been there. It can be stressful because your mom is upset you're not spending time with her. Similarly, if your host has a noisy household (even though you're sequestered in a room), it might be better to have a writing retreat elsewhere.

Caveats aside, these retreats are wonderful when you

demonstrate how much you've accomplished thanks to your host! It gives them a concrete way to support you rather than giving you that glazed-over listening look when you tell them how many papers you need to write.

As is the case with all writing retreats, planning ahead is important. Please bring your own food or snacks because you may think you can eat what's there or get sucked into a three-hour lunch with your host. Or there may not be anything in the house! Pack a bag with all of your essentials (see tips at the end for more information).

4. Conference Extension

Budget: Free (reimbursed) to $$

Ideal for these intentions:

- Start a project—get going
- Butt-in-chair drafting
- Finish and submit
- Need space with authors to work on a project

Less ideal for these intentions:

- Assess and Reflect on big-picture goals (e.g., tenure file)

- Learn/practice a new writing skill

We've used this strategy with great results. Try tacking on a few days before or after a conference as your writing retreat. Depending on your faculty/graduate student funding, you can get these extra days reimbursed, or you can at least get the travel costs reimbursed. If you're meeting with a co-author who doesn't live near you, use that rationale for reimbursement. Or, you could attend a workshop or conference covered by a grant and decide to tack on a few more days. Worst case scenario, you can arrive a day early and stay a day late, and no one will question the reimbursement.

When creating an extension retreat, you must be realistic about the conference itself. Will you go to all the sessions and then crash immediately after the conference? Is your presentation scheduled for the first conference day so you have plenty of time to recover before your writing retreat? Or, conversely, are you scheduled to speak at eight on Sunday morning (we're sorry) at the end of the conference? If so, planning a few days before the conference might make more sense. In general, adding days *after* the conference rather than prior to it may be a better strategy to avoid having the presentation hanging over you while you write.

As we note above, extension retreats are ideal for focused writing rather than planning or learning. If you're short on cash, move to a cheaper hotel by the airport, for example. You won't be tempted by the sights outside the hotel and will focus on the writing tasks at hand.

If you are in a particularly beautiful or interesting place, however, you could plan for a reflection retreat that involves a combination of sightseeing and short, focused writing/brainstorming sessions in a cafe. The point is to plan your intentions ahead of time.

5. Hotel or Rental

Budget: Free (reimbursed) to $$$

Ideal for these intentions:

- Start a project—get going
- Butt-in-chair drafting
- Finish and submit
- Need space with authors to work on a project
- Assess and Reflect on big-picture goals (e.g., tenure file)
- Learn/practice a new writing skill

We need not dwell on this type of retreat as it provides the most options. Whether you choose a short-term rental or a hotel, location is possibly the most important factor.

In the Woods or on the Water

This retreat is ideal for rejuvenation, reflection, and planning. Whatever kind of natural environment speaks to you, this retreat offers the opportunity for long walks and healing. If you've had a tough semester or academic year, this might be what you need.

These retreats are also useful in accomplishing specific writing tasks but be careful not to over-schedule or set your sights too high. Otherwise, you'll be plagued by a sense of time slipping away and high anxiety over what you are not accomplishing. Once you accept that healing and rest is the goal, the words are more likely to flow.

Apartment or Hotel in a City

If your university or college is in a sleepy rural town, a trip to the city might be just what you need! Perhaps you're feeling stuck or lack motivation. Temporarily living in a new neighborhood can bring a fresh perspective that will spark new ideas and break through old mental blocks.

6. Retreat Center

Budget: Free (reimbursed) to $$$

Ideal for these intentions:

- Start a project—get going
- Butt-in-chair drafting
- Finish and submit
- Need space with authors to work on a project
- Assess and Reflect on big-picture goals (e.g., tenure file)
- Learn/practice a new writing skill

Retreat centers are a fantastic option for writers because they are specifically designed for reflection and productivity. Often, they will provide needed supplies such as large desks, comfortable chairs, and printers. You'll want to research the center carefully before you go, however, and not make assumptions about what is provided.

Some retreat centers offer meals, while others provide cooking spaces. Either way, you'll want to decide if you're going to build in cooking as a relaxing time for you or if you're planning on bringing ready-made-meals and/or eating out. We enjoy making simple, quick meals or bringing already-prepared food so it's one less thing for us to decide for the day.

Another aspect of retreat centers you'll want to research are expectations around interactions with other writers.

Some retreat centers have communal meals or time together at various points in the day. If you think socializing time will be a welcome break to your day, then by all means select these kinds of retreat centers. For others, these planned events can become somewhat bothersome if you are in the middle of a flow state and do not want interruptions.

Retreat centers are also ideal for working with a co-author or simply going with a friend/colleague on a writing retreat together. It is doubly important the two of you (or more) plan ahead carefully, even if you just talk in the car on the way to the retreat. Everyone has different writing rhythms, and it is critical that you understand those before you go on retreat. For example, if you're a morning writer and your colleague is a night owl, then you will be frustrated when they haven't accomplished much during the day. In this morning/night scenario, you could write your morning portion and hand it off to your colleague to finish in the evening—then you have something ready for the following morning.

Finally, established center retreats are often easier to get reimbursed than hotel or apartment rentals. Retreat centers often have an application process to become a 'fellow' while you're there, which is yet another line on your CV!

. . .

7. Some Facilitated Retreats (Caution)

Budget: Free (reimbursed) to $$$

Ideal for these intentions:

- Assess and Reflect on big-picture goals (e.g., tenure file)
- Learn/practice a new writing skill

Less ideal for these intentions:

- Start a project—get going
- Butt-in-chair drafting
- Finish and submit
- Need space with authors to work on a project

A facilitated retreat can be both the most frustrating and the most rewarding kind of writing retreat experience. Unlike other retreat types, *someone else* sets the agenda, not you.

Frustrating!

How could a writing retreat in a beautiful location with delicious meals and a gracious host be frustrating? The answer is conflicting expectations. Much like a vacation where you want maximum relaxation and rest, while going sightseeing for ten hours a day, you'll end up feeling neither rested nor energized. If you arrive at a facilitated retreat with maximum rest in mind, as well as writing your entire book, you'll be sorely disappointed. Be sure to research these retreats to ensure they match your needs. While accomplishing a specific writing task can be a side benefit, if the facilitated retreat is filled with meditation, meals, writing critique circles, and leaves only 45 minutes a day for writing, you'll be frustrated by lack of writing progress. If, on the other hand, you accept a goal of reflecting on your scholarly trajectory or a new project, then you'll be pleasantly surprised.

Rewarding!

Facilitated retreats can provide soul-rest as well as space to reconnect with the reasons you joined the academy. You may realize what is holding you back from making writing progress. You may learn a new writing technique. You may feel supported by a community of like-minded scholars. That energy is invaluable, and if you treat it as such, you'll be itching to return next year.

12

OPTIONS FOR INSPIRATIONAL RETREATS

Here are the best options for an inspirational retreat.

1. Facilitated Retreats

Budget: Free (reimbursed) to $$$

Facilitated inspirational retreats provide spaces to deepen one's writing practice in a supportive environment. Whether your goal is to reinvigorate your writing, find accountability and inspiration, make substantial progress on a manuscript, or anything in between, there is probably a facilitated writing retreat available to meet your needs.

What's critical to your gaining your desired outcomes is

identifying what you want to gain from the retreat. These are an investment of time and resources to make sure the retreat is in line with your needs and aspirations.

Here's our facilitated retreat options overview.

Online

There are numerous formats of online writing retreats to inspire your writing process. Some provide regular spaces for virtual co-writing and peer support. Angelique's Exhale: Online Writing Retreats meets every Friday from 9am-1pm PST/12pm-4pm EST to share inspiration for the day, writing goals, accountability, accompaniment, and encouragement. These are facilitated through Zoom. After a brief introduction that includes an inspirational message and tip for the day, there are timed writing sprints with breaks for troubleshooting and support with other participants. Faculty from around the country participate and look forward to this time each week. Many of them know each other from various professional organizations and look forward to this opportunity to connect, outside of the conference circuit, on a regular basis.

There are other forms of online writing retreats as well. Inkwell provides periodic "Still I Write" online retreats free of charge. These half-day retreats provide the opportunity to enter a protected writing space, with a community of scholars, and the support of an expert writing coach. Cathy Mazak also provides co-writing opportunities through her Academic Women's Write Collective. Outside the academy, numerous groups support writers such as "Shut Up and Write Tuesdays," or Creative Nonfiction group coaching co-writing sessions.

In-person Facilitated Writing Retreats

In-person writing retreats provide the opportunity to work in physical proximity to others, share goals and ideas, and also for support and inspiration.

Angelique facilitates in-person writing retreats called Exhale: Pause & Reset Academic Writing Retreats. She created these as a response to academics' never-ending scholarship, teaching, service, and personal 'to do' lists. They pause participants' 'to do' lists by protecting time for substantial progress on a writing project. They also provide an opportunity to reset their 'to do' list through creating space to reframe the best way to approach to the never-ending demands on their time.

In addition to a lush resort setting and opportunity to experience the local culture, history, and cuisine, this retreat also includes developmental editing sessions, daily guided meditation sessions, and individual coaching sessions focused on tailoring how writing retreats can increase your scholarly productivity and make space for the rest of your life.

This retreat is designed to support those who self-identify as women of color and their allies. Although developed based on the needs of those in the academy, it is suitable for those in other professions who endeavor to make significant progress on a substantial writing project(s).

There are many other formats of facilitated writing retreats to participate in. While all create space from the academic roller-coaster, there are a multiplicity of options to choose from to meet your needs. Some like Michelle Boyd's Composed Residential Writing Retreats for Scholars and Cathy Mazak's Academic Women's Writing Retreats also provide coaching on academic writing and career development. Others such as WellAcademic's Women of Color Academic Retreats provide facilitated activities designed to help one replenish from systemic, institutional, and individual challenges (See the comprehensive list at end of the book).

In-Person Facilitated Conference Retreats

Another option for in-person retreats includes those adjacent to a conference. One example is the pre-and post-workshop writing retreat for Lutie A. Lytle Writing Workshop participants that Angelique has assisted facilitating. This is scheduled one day before and four days after the yearly workshop. The goal is to create space to make progress on writing projects while being in community with others. Meals are provided so participants can focus on their writing. Group meals and breaks also offer the opportunity for feedback and support.

Other organizations also host pre and post-conference writing retreats. This can be an excellent way to extend your travel budget and incorporate a writing retreat at the same time.

Facilitated Campus Retreats

Some universities offer internal or externally facilitated writing retreats. These range from a partial day to several days in length with their scope varying from those focused solely on writing to other forms of professional development. Typically these involve general sessions with writing tips and strategies as well as protected space for writing where details such as meals, minimized distractions, and a comfortable environment are provided. Some campus retreats are regularly scheduled, and others are singular activities. These are typically low cost to the participant and offer another avenue to consider in your retreat repertoire.

2. DIY

Budget: Free (reimbursed) to $$

You can create a DIY inspiration retreat online or in person. To create one online, you can use several software platforms such as Zoom, FaceTime, Skype, or Google Hangouts to write in community with others. Another option to add inspiration to your writing practice is to create a DIY in-person inspiration writing retreat that centers your professional wellbeing, creativity, and an opportunity to focus on why you are doing this work. There may be a book, course, podcast, or other inspirational materials that you wish to finish reading and incorporate into your practice. You may need space to contemplate all the moving pieces in your world and determine your next steps. Whatever the need, you can also design your own retreat to add inspiration and space for writing. These can take place on your own or in community with others. The space options are also endless and really dependent on your circumstances. Hotels, friends or family, as well as retreat centers, are all excellent places to retreat. We outline practical tips for DIY retreats including sample schedules in later sections.

3. Retreat Centers

Budget: Free (reimbursed) to $$$

Retreat Centers across the country offer dedicated space for writing. They span the creative and professional spectrum, with some solely devoted to writers. In our resources section, we provide a list writing retreat centers we are familiar with. Some of these centers offer facilitated retreats, but most provide space to write and interact over meals with other writers. Many of these require applications, so they must be planned in advance. Make sure to check each location's guidelines.

PART VI

CONCLUSION

13

ROSE'S STORY

May 25, 2019.

Writing retreats helped me arrive at one of the most important decisions of my life: to leave my position as chair and associate professor of political science in less than a month. To leave academia and become an academic editor, consultant, and coach. And a fiction author.

Academia can be a toxic place, especially those who experience daily injustice and those who fight against it. It has taken a toll on my health. I credit writing retreats with allowing me the space to breathe and carry on.

Spending time by myself, and with Angelique at the Whiteley Center, allowed me the mental space to realize it was time to start a new chapter in my life. One that was still connected to academia, but outside the institution rather than inside it. Working with scholars one-on-one has always been my passion, one that was difficult to achieve amidst the politics and bureaucracy of the institution. Now I can support critical scholars in producing scholarship that needs to be shared with the world.

Regardless of whether you're a graduate student contemplating working outside academia or a tenured professor excited about applying for full professor, these retreats will be invaluable in bringing more joy into your life.

Though I am leaving academia, I will never leave behind these retreats.

See you at the Whiteley Center!

Would you like to receive our packing checklist? Sign up here to receive the checklist and occasional updates about sparking academic joy.

PART VII

SAMPLE SCHEDULES

TRIAGE SAMPLE SCHEDULES

We've put together two sample schedules for a triage retreat.

1. Online

This schedule is based on Angelique's *Exhale: Online Academic Writing Retreats* that take place each week and are four hours long.

00:00-0:05 Opening

00:05-0:30 Sprint #1

0:30-0:35 Break

0:35-01:00 Sprint #2

01:00-01:05 Break

01:05-01:30 Sprint #3

01:30-01:35 Break

01:35-02:00 Sprint #4

02:00-02:30 Long Break

02:30-02:55 Sprint #5

02:55-03:00 Break

03:00-03:25 Sprint #6

03:25-03:30 Break

03:30-03:55 Sprint #7

03:55-04:00 Closing

Often opening sessions are used to share writing goals or other writing tips and inspiration for this day.

2. Local Weekend Triage AWAY from Home:

Day 1

04:00-07:00pm Travel to Retreat Destination and Get Settled

07:00-08:00pm Goal Setting and Getting Organized

08:00-? Writing Sprints (25-minute sessions followed by a 5-minute break)

Day 2 (repeat as needed)

07:00-08:00am Exercise

08:00-09:00am Breakfast

09:00-12:00pm Writing Sprints

12:00-02:00pm Lunch Break w/ Rejuvenating Activity (walk, nap, meditation, etc.)

02:00-06:00pm Writing Sprints

06:00-07:00pm Dinner

07:00-08:00pm Review Work and Set Goal(s) for the Next Day

08:00-? Rewarding Activity (Netflix, reading, listening to audiobook, etc.)

Last Day

07:00-08:00am Exercise

08:00-09:00am Breakfast

09:00-11:00pm Writing Sprints

11:00-12:00pm Review Work and Set Goal(s) to For Return Home

Check-Out of Hotel

This retreat is formulated for a weekend Friday through Sunday triage retreat; however, it can be adjusted depending upon your needs. Day 2 can be repeated as many times as necessary depending upon the length of your retreat. The hours also should be adjusted to match your own circadian rhythms.

15

PROACTIVE SAMPLE SCHEDULES

We've put together two sample schedules for a proactive retreat.

1. Online

The following is a sample 4-hour online morning/early afternoon retreat.

Day Before

- Plan intentions.
- Plan to minimize distractions for the retreat (let family know and turn off internet distractions; finish any pressing tasks). This is especially important because you need to have the internet on during the retreat.

- Get some sleep!
- Prepare some treats for yourself.

Day of Online Retreat

Before:

- Make yourself a favorite beverage.
- Get comfortable.
- Remind anyone in the house that you're on retreat (this includes feeding pets so they don't show up with sad eyes).

During:

- Hydrate.
- Focus, knowing you have a small break and treat coming.

2. Local

Day Before

- Decide on a place where you'll work.
- Plan on arriving early or at a time when you'll be sure to get a seat!
- Plan intentions.

Decide if this is going to be a timed retreat or a results retreat:

- Timed retreats are ideal for designing, editing, or finishing projects. This means that after you've completed 6 pomodoros, for example, your retreat is over.
- Results retreats are ideal for butt-in-chair drafting. For example, if you know exactly what you need to write (and you just need to write it), then set yourself a word-count goal of 3,000 words, for example. This encourages you just to write, especially if you are challenged by your inner critic during the drafting stage. If you use timers, on the other hand, you may just stare out the window until the timer is done and then leave your retreat feeling frustrated.
- Prepare a bag with all of your materials: power cord, noise canceling headphones, paper, pens, and any research materials you need.
- Get some sleep!
- Prepare some treats for yourself.

During:

- Hydrate
- Focus on your task, knowing you have a small break and treat coming.

INSPIRE SAMPLE SCHEDULES

We've put together two sample schedules for an inspirational retreat.

1. Group Residential Retreats

This sample schedule is based upon Angelique's *Exhale: Pause & Reset Academic writing* five-day writing retreats. Other facilitated retreats use varying formats that you can often find on the facilitator's website.

Day 1

04:00-07:00pm Check-in, Explore & Relax

07:00-09:00pm Welcome Gathering & Goal Setting

Day 2: Writing Intensive Day (repeat as needed)

07:00-08:00am Group Exercise and/or Meditation

08:00-09:00am Continental Breakfast

09:00-12:00pm Writing Session (25-minute sessions followed by a 5-minute break)

12:00-01:00pm Catered Lunch

01:00-04:00pm Writing Session

04:00-06:00pm Coaching & Developmental Editing Sessions

06:00-08:00pm Dinner at Local Restaurant

Day 3: Writing and Exploration Day (repeat as needed)

07:00-08:00am Group Exercise and/or Meditation

08:00-09:00am Continental Breakfast

09:00-12:00pm Writing Session

12:00-01:00pm Lunch at Local Restaurant

01:00-04:00pm Local Excursion/Activity

04:00-06:00pm Coaching & Developmental Editing Sessions

06:00-08:00pm Dinner at Local Restaurant

Last day

07:00-08:00am Group Exercise and/or Meditation

08:00-09:00am Continental Breakfast

09:00-11:00am Writing Session

11:00-12:00pm Review Work and Set Goal(s) For Return Home

12:00-12:30pm Check Out of Hotel

12:30-02:30pm Closing Lunch/Brunch

2. Individual Retreats

This sample scheduled is a template to help you get started if you're doing an individual writing retreat.

Day 1

04:00-07:00pm Check-Into Hotel, Explore & Relax

07:00-08:00pm Goal Setting

Day 2: Writing Intensive Day (repeat as needed)

07:00-08:00am Exercise and/or Meditation

08:00-09:00am Breakfast

09:00-12:00pm Writing Sprints (25-minute sessions followed by a 5-minute break)

12:00-01:00pm Lunch

01:00-04:00pm Writing Sprints

04:00-06:00pm Personal Development

06:00-08:00pm Dinner

08:00-? Rewarding Activity (Netflix, reading, listen to audiobook, etc.)

Day 3: Writing and Exploration Day (repeat as needed)

07:00-08:00am Exercise and/or Meditation

08:00-09:00am Breakfast

09:00-12:00pm Writing Sprints

12:00-01:00pm Lunch at Local Restaurant

01:00-04:00pm Local Excursion/Activity

04:00-06:00pm Personal Development

06:00-08:00pm Dinner at Local Restaurant

Last Day

07:00-08:00am Exercise and/or Meditation

08:00-09:00am Breakfast

09:00-11:00pm Writing Sprints

11:00-12:00pm Review Work and Set Goal(s) For Return Home

Check-Out of Hotel

PART VIII

TIPS FOR A SUCCESSFUL RETREAT

17

ANGELIQUE'S TIPS FOR A JOYFUL RETREAT

Before the retreat, you'll want to consider these possibilities.

- *Block out the time on your calendar!* Treat this like any other work commitment and protect this time. Do it in advance so you can arrange for "coverage" while you're away!
- *Identify your goal.* What is your overall goal for the retreat?
- *Once you've determined your goal, work backward and map how you are going to complete your project in the amount of time available.* Depending upon your project, this may or may not include time outside of the scheduled retreat. An excellent resource for this is the National Center for Faculty Development and Diversity's

(NCFDD's) strategic planning and semester plan resources. Whatever you do, take the time you think you will need to complete each project and multiply it by 3. We all know that writing takes MUCH longer than planned!

- *Compile the research you need for each retreat session ahead of time.* This will help you focus on writing.
- *Gather the necessary items.* For some, this includes soundproof headphones, a hot beverage, a warm blanket, or lighting a candle. You catch my drift. Make sure to gather all of these items together ahead of time, so they are ready for the retreat session.
- *If you are a caregiver plan the necessary coverage of your care-taking responsibilities well in advance!*
- *For online retreats, identify and prepare your writing location.* Identify where you are going to write. In your home office? Work office? A coffee shop? Library? Keep in mind that you need a location where interruptions will be minimized. This is a time to be realistic. If people typically interrupt you in your campus office finding another place will most likely be better. Do you need to clean your office? Is it so full of clutter that it distracts from your writing? If so, set aside some time to prepare your office.

At the retreat:

- *Set Boundaries.* Be realistic about distractions! Minimize them by letting others know ahead of time that you are working. If Wi-Fi is a challenge for you, select a location with no Wi-Fi, turn it off, or use some other type of internet blocker. Carefully choose your location. If people continuously interrupt you at your selected location, consider finding another space where you won't be interrupted.
- *Use writing sprints.* Most people know these from the Pomodoro Technique developed by Francesco Cirillo. The idea is that you do writing sprints, followed by short breaks to help increase your productivity and focus. Typically after four 25-minute sprints, followed by five-minute breaks, you take a longer break.
- *Break up your day.* Walks. Naps. Coffee. Shopping. You name it. Take a break to recharge and catch your second wind.
- *Reward yourself each day!* Catch up on a television series, read a book, go to bed early, you name it!

After the retreat:

- *Schedule your next retreat.* At the end of your retreat or immediately thereafter. Don't just think about it, put it on your calendar, and book your accommodations.
- *If you created a plan while on your retreat, stick to it!* Place it somewhere you'll see it often and refer to it on a regular basis.

ROSE'S TIPS FOR A JOYFUL RETREAT

Before the retreat, you'll want to consider these possibilities.

- *Clear digital clutter.* In addition to setting intentions before you go, make sure your desktop (whichever device you're taking with you) is clear and organized. This not only contributes to a sense of calm when you arrive but will cut down on possible distractions in finding the right document or file for you to work on the first day of your retreat.
- *Pack favorite beverages.* I bring plenty of tea and coffee.
- *Pack a journal.* Who knows? You may be inspired!

- *Prepare playlists and background sounds.* In addition to preparing whatever music you like to listen to in the background while working (if it works for you), you might also find sound generators. My favorite is mynoise.net. I also like to download podcasts for walks.
- *Comfortable clothing.* Unless you plan to go clubbing every night, we suggest you bring as much comfortable clothing as possible.
- *Prepare meals ahead of time.* Shop in advance if you can do that and plan for simple meals.
- *Bring your favorite snacks!* Enough said.
- *Bring things from home that make you feel at home.* This depends on whether you're flying somewhere or not, but I always like to bring a string of fairy/Christmas lights with me to set up in the space.
- *Set intentions and boundaries with friends, family, and work. It's* important to know this for yourself and for others so they don't distract you—or you don't seek them out as distractions yourself!

At the retreat:

- *Set intentions the night before.* It's important that you wake up and feel ready to face the day. A blank schedule can be overwhelming to academics who are used to having our lives over-scheduled! Even if the schedule is to take walks and naps, it's important that you know that so you'll enjoy them!
- *Take lots of walks.* You may not be able to walk, but the point is to move in whatever way feels good to you.
- *Take naps.* I love to rise early and work until late morning. Then I take a long shower, eat lunch, take a walk, and sometimes take a nap (not necessarily in that order). Then I'm ready to work for a few more hours in the afternoon.
- *Do something fun/relaxing at night.* Angelique and I often like to end our day around 7pm with dinner and a delicious TV show. Reward yourself!
- *Be flexible.* It's important to take detours at a retreat (depending on what kind it is) and be flexible. I'd lovingly ask you not to confuse this with resistance and distraction, however.

After the retreat:

- *Celebrate your accomplishments!* This is something that is difficult for me to do, but is easier after a retreat because I'm usually astonished by what I've accomplished.
- *Plan for your next retreat!*

PART IX

RESOURCES AND FURTHER READING

19

EXHALE: ONLINE WRITING RETREATS

Exhale. Set aside time for your writing. Most of us have regular writing routines yet wish for a longer stretch of time to focus our thoughts and write in community with others. These are, of course, elusive with the hectic nature of our everyday lives. So…treat this like a meeting. Block out the time on your calendar, let people know you won't be available because you're working. Have to teach? Juggling daycare? Whether you're running late or need to leave early, this retreat is several hours so you can join as your schedule permits and still get in a substantial chunk of writing time. Give yourself the gift of half a day to write in community with others. You deserve this!

After a brief introduction that includes an inspirational message and tip for the day, we will jump into timed writing sprints with breaks for troubleshooting and support with other participants. Writing sprints will begin on the half hour, and you are welcome to join as your schedule permits. In addition, you will be given prompts to help you explore more deeply why you write. To help you tap into why you started doing this type of work in the first place.

Join us. Make these a part of your writing routine. End your term knowing you've accomplished something!

20

EXHALE: PAUSE & RESET ACADEMIC WRITING RETREATS

As a Professor of Color, wife, and mother of four, I often fantasize about having metaphorical *pause* and *reset* buttons. When I push *pause*: the world around me stops, I complete my never-ending scholarship, teaching, service, and personal 'to do' list, and sometimes I even get ahead. If things are too chaotic, I hit *reset*: my 'to do' list resets to my usual list of activities, and the backlog is erased. Ironically, I am penalized for indulging this fantasy—by taking time off work, I return to an even longer list. I'm guessing you can relate.

Over the past 15 years, I've utilized writing retreats to pause and reset. My quarterly retreats allow me to work smarter, not harder. I use them to augment my daily writing practice (I utilize the method created by the National Center for Faculty Development and Diversity). They pause my 'to do' list by protecting time for substantial progress on a writing project. They reset my 'to do' list by giving me space to reframe the best way to approach to the never-ending demands on my time.

In addition to a lush resort setting and opportunity to experience the local culture, history, and cuisine, the retreat also includes developmental editing sessions with Rose Ernst, daily guided meditation sessions, and individual coaching sessions focused on individually tailoring how writing retreats can increase your scholarly productivity and make space for the rest of your life. And a glass of wine.

This retreat is designed to support those who self-identify as women of color and their allies. Although developed based on the needs of those in the academy, it is suitable for those in other professions who endeavor to make significant progress on a major writing project(s).

I have facilitated writing retreats for both small and large groups over the past 10 years. Some have been for small groups of faculty that provided structured feedback sessions in addition to large blocks of dedicated writing time.

For more information, visit my website or contact me at angelique@angeliquemdavis.com.

21

OTHER ORGANIZED RETREATS

Academic Bootcamp Retreats, Professors and Graduate Students (various, UK)

http://www.quillout.com/

Academic Women's Writing Retreat (Puerto Rico, USA)

https://www.cathymazak.com/writing-retreat/

Anchorage Education: Writing Retreats for Academic Writing (Various)

http://anchorage-education.co.uk/#

. . .

Artisa Academic & Art Retreat (Greece)

https://artisagreece.org/

Center for Research and Education on Women & Work (Ontario, Canada)

https://carleton.ca/creww/writing-retreat/

Chapelgarth Academic Writing Retreat (North Yorkshire, UK)

https://www.chapelgarth-estate.co.uk/retreats

Hope Springs Institute Academic Writing Retreat (Ohio, USA)

http://www.hopespringsinstitute.org/academicwriting.html

Inkwell Retreats (Various)

https://www.inkwellretreats.org/

. . .

Risman Writing Retreat (Illinois, USA)

http://www.barbararisman.com/rismans-writing-retreats.html

Structured Writing Retreats (Helsinki, Finland)

https://www.writingretreat.fi/

22

RETREAT CENTERS

Note: Some of these retreats are geared toward fiction writers rather than academic writers; we've included them, however, as academics may apply.

Artsmith Residency Fellows (Washington, USA)

http://orcasartsmith.org/index.html

Bellagio Center for Academic Writing Residency (Bellagio, Italy)

https://www.rockefellerfoundation.org/our-work/bellagio-center/residency-program/academic-writing-residency/

. . .

Campos de Gutiérrez (Medellin, Colombia)

http://camposdegutierrez.org/residencies/stays/

Gullkistan Residency (Iceland)

http://gullkistan.is/

Hedgebrook (Washington, USA)

https://hedgebrook.org/writers-in-residence/

Lacawac Writing Retreat for Academics (Pennsylvania, USA)

https://www.lacawac.org/writing-retreat.html

Le Choisel Writing Retreat (Normandy, France)

https://lechoisel.com/academic-writing-retreat-in-normandy

MacDowell Fellowship Residency (New Hampshire, USA)

https://www.macdowellcolony.org/

. . .

Urban Writers Retreat (various, UK)

http://www.urbanwritersretreat.co.uk/a-residential-writing-retreat/

Wellspring House (Massachusetts, USA)

https://wellspringhouseretreat.com/

Wellstone Center in the Redwoods (California, USA)

http://www.wellstoneredwoods.org/

Whiteley Center (Washington, USA)

https://fhl.uw.edu/facilities-resources/whiteley-center/

Willapa Bay AiR (Washington, USA)

http://www.willapabayair.org/

23
RECOMMENDED BOOKS

Becoming an Academic Writer. By Patricia Goodson

https://us.sagepub.com/en-us/nam/becoming-an-academic-writer/book244337

The Black Academic's Guide to Winning Tenure—Without Losing Your Soul.

By Kerry Ann Rockquemore and Tracey Laszloffy

https://www.rienner.com/title/The_Black_Academic_s_Guide_to_Winning_Tenure_Without_Losing_Your_Soul

Coaches Guide for Women Professors. By Rena Seltzer

http://www.leaderacademic.com/the-coachs-guide/

A Clockwork Muse: A Practical Guide to Writing Theses, Dissertations, and Books. By Eviatar Zerubavel

http://www.hup.harvard.edu/catalog.php?isbn=9780674135864

Fast-Draft Your Memoir. Rachel Herron.

https://rachaelherron.com/books/memoir/fast-draft-your-memoir/

Flow: The Psychology of Optimal Experience. Mihaly Csikszentmihalyi

https://www.harpercollins.com/9780061339202/flow/

Getting It Published. By William Germano

https://press.uchicago.edu/ucp/books/book/chicago/G/bo23290957.html

Playing Big. Tara Mohr

https://www.taramohr.com/the-playing-big-book/

The Power of Habit: Why We Do What We Do in Life and Business. Charles Duhigg

https://charlesduhigg.com/the-power-of-habit/

Rest: Why You Get More Done When You Work Less. By Alex Soojung-Kim Pang

https://www.basicbooks.com/titles/alex-soojung-kim-pang/rest/9781478988762/

Stop Worrying, Start Writing. By Sarah Painter

https://www.sarah-painter.com/books/stop-worrying-start-writing/

Stylish Academic Writing. By Helen Sword

http://www.hup.harvard.edu/catalog.php?isbn=9780674064485

Tricks of the Trade: How to Think About Your Research While You're Doing it. By Howard S. Becker https://www.press.uchicago.edu/ucp/books/book/chicago/T/bo3683418.html

Write No Matter What. By Joli Jenson

https://press.uchicago.edu/ucp/books/book/chicago/W/bo26049293.html

The Writer's Diet. By Helen Sword

https://www.press.uchicago.edu/ucp/books/book/chicago/W/bo23162311.html

Writing Your Journal Article in Twelve Weeks: A Guide to Academic Publishing Success. By Wendy Belcher

https://wendybelcher.com/writing-advice/writing-your-journal-article-in-twelve/

24
RETREAT DATABASES

Artist Residencies: Arteles (includes writers)
https://www.arteles.org/residency.html#apply

Association of Writers and Writing Programs

https://www.awpwriter.org/wcc/directory_conferences_centers

Poets & Writers Conferences and Residencies Database

https://www.pw.org/conferences_and_residencies

Rivet

https://rivet.es/calls/

Upcoming Writers Conferences & Writing Workshops Events

http://writing.shawguides.com/Events

The Writers' Retreat

http://www.writersretreat.com/

25
ARTICLES, BLOGS AND ADDITIONAL RESOURCES

Academic Muse

https://academicmuse.org/

Explorations of Style: A blog about academic writing

https://explorationsofstyle.com/

Hunks, Chunks, & Bites

https://meggin.com/classes/hunks-chunks-bites/

Improving Your Academic Writing: My Top 10 Tips; Raul Pacheco-Vega http://www.raulpacheco.org/2013/02/improving-your-academic-writing-my-top-10-tips/

InkWell Blog

https://www.inkwellretreats.org/read

"Just Think: The Challenges of the Disengaged Mind." By Timothy D. Wilson, David A. Reinhard, Erin C. Westgate, Daniel T. Gilbert, Nicole Ellerbeck, Cheryl Hahn, Casey L. Brown, and Adi Shaked. *Social Pyschology*

https://wjh-www.harvard.edu/~dtg/WILSON%20ET%20AL%202014.pdf

"My Writing Productivity Pipeline." Erin Marie Furtak.

https://www.chronicle.com/article/My-Writing-Productivity/236712

Patter: Research Education, Academic Writing, Public Engagement, Funding, Other Eccentricities

https://patthomson.net/

. . .

"Pay Yourself First." By Kerry Ann Rockquemore

https://www.insidehighered.com/advice/2010/11/01/pay-yourself-first

The Professor is In (plus book)

http://theprofessorisin.com/

Research Degree Insiders

https://researchinsiders.blog/2013/03/12/stages-of-writing/

The Research Whisperer

https://theresearchwhisperer.wordpress.com/

Struggling with Structure? Break Out the Scissors

https://chroniclevitae.com/news/458-struggling-with-structure-break-out-the-scissors

Tara Mohr Blog

https://www.taramohr.com/

. . .

The Thesis Whisperer

https://thesiswhisperer.com/2012/12/12/turn-your-notes-into-writing-using-the-cornell-method/

This Itch of Writing

https://emmadarwin.typepad.com/thisitchofwriting/

Write, Publish, Thrive! A Blog About Writing, Publishing, and the Scholarly Life

http://writepublishthrive.blogspot.com/

Writer's Diet Diagnostic Tool (favorite)

http://writersdiet.com/

PACKING CHECKLIST

Would you like to receive our packing checklist? Sign up here to receive the checklist and occasional updates about sparking academic joy.

ABOUT THE AUTHORS

Angelique M. Davis is Associate Professor of Political Science and Director of Global African Studies at Seattle University. As a tenured professor, attorney, and mother of four—as well as coach for the National Center for Faculty Development and Diversity and facilitator of writing retreats—she gained unique insights into the gratifications and frustrations of the academic writing and publication process. She practiced law until she joined the faculty at Seattle University in 2005. In addition to her academic pursuits, Professor Davis remains a licensed attorney in Washington state and chairs the Seattle Civil Service Commission. Find her at: https://angeliquemdavis.com.

Rose Ernst is an academic editor, writing consultant, and coach. She served as Chair and Associate Professor of Political Science at Seattle University until 2019. She received her PhD from the University of Washington and BA from Cornell University. As an author, Rose understands the joys and challenges of academic writing and publishing. NYU Press published her first book, *The Price of Progressive Politics: The Welfare Rights Movement in an Era of Colorblind Racism* (2010). She has also published articles in many acclaimed social science journals. As a developmental editor and writing coach, she specializes in the social sciences, history, law, interdisciplinary social sciences/humanities, and research ethics. Rose is always seeking ways to improve writing routines, dance with writing resistance, and support scholars in producing and publishing their best work. Email her at rose@roseernst.net.

Copyright © 2019 by Angelique M. Davis and Rose Ernst

First published in 2019 by Alchemy House Press

https://angeliquemdavis.com/

https://roseernst.net/

All rights reserved. No part of this book may be reproduced or transmitted in any form or by any means, electronic or mechanical, including photocopying, recording, or by any information storage and retrieval system without the written permission of the publisher, except where permitted by law.

Alchemy House Press

Unceded Duwamish Land

Seattle, Washington